# EMOJI REVIVAL

I0169666

MARZI MARGO

Be About It Press

**Be About It Press @baipress**
**May 2022**

cover design by David Wojciechowski
@MrWojoRising

edited by Alexandra Naughton
@hegemonster

# CONTENTS

"I can only write poetry that is like a tuba covered with blood…"

- Chelsey Minnis, "Preface 4"

"Picture me swinging a golf club

while I write this. It's humiliating,

the fear of direction…"

- Ava Wolf, "Swing and a Miss"

# MOBILE TELEVISION (A)

the stars

freezing


non vodka

non lemon twist


neither either/or nor ether

airship international


animal tracking basics

akimbo


a purple pencil in her sight

& in her inner hand


peach tea tree leaves

sunlight simulating transition

# MOBILE TELEVISION (B)

pop gun suicide

gone wild out west


circular birds

permanent geranium lake


crowds as communities

streetlights as symbols


contemporary burial

drawn to the dusk


scraped sky

color building perception


my gender is to slime

as slime is to my essence

# SOLSTICE SONNET (SUMMER)

city of gerunds

the verdant sun

cameras like diamonds flashing

policing my protection

myriad greens

zune stone

cum laude mistress

the asemic writing of gender

neosporin diet

isolated schism

paint by numbness

the sculpture guides the sculptor

dishwasher with dishwater

hyperlink forgotten by history

# SOLSTICE SONNET (WINTER)

quaalude symphony

grammar as jingoism

hikikomori fetish

super mario world war

open sesame season

lobster fried rice

united states of a miracle

ghosts & sriracha

loss is key

the building

friendly to strangers

the revolution will not be

starshine

cosmic phenomenology or something like it

# WE ARE ONLY AS WE ARE

*may 2020*

safe wishes to the reynolds wrap & electrical tape that keeps my broken air conditioner secured in my windowsill. safe wishes to the little brown spiders who live in that windowsill's corners. safe wishes to the pink plastic piano on the floor next to my desk. safe wishes to my desk that's actually an outdoor folding table from walmart. safe wishes to the tiny hot wheels figurine of professional skateboarder steve caballero that i recently shoplifted from the grocery store where i work. safe wishes to the many, many cans of soup at my workplace that have been collecting soft layers of dust for months & will never be purchased by anyone. safe wishes to the decaf coffee that nobody wants to buy or drink in the midst of a pandemic. safe wishes to my coworker who is twice my age & rants about the federal government injecting covid-19 patients with a mind-control microchip while we both stock boxes of cereal. safe wishes to apple jacks. safe wishes to the doctor who prescribes me my estrogen. safe wishes to the people who just burned down a police station in minneapolis (fuck yeah). safe wishes to my friends. safe wishes to all the sufferers. safe wishes to what the idea of home used to be & how it used to feel. safe wishes to gillian anderson.

# MOVIES DIRECTED BY AMY HECKERLING

*april 2020*

i'm methodically extracting teeth from the mouth of a river & placing each one neatly at the foot of a bed, sized california king. someone sleeps in the bed & will step on all the river teeth when the time is right. but after that someone wakes up & before they get out of bed, they will spend approximately five hours playing animal crossing: new horizons on their nintendo switch lite, pulling virtual weeds & collecting virtual seashells & talking to virtual neighbors & shaking virtual trees & running from the virtual wasps who descend from those virtual trees. the someone in bed will be blissfully unaware of the carefully collected teeth waiting to make contact with the soles of their feet. but when the feet do meet the teeth, the someone will be delighted by the feeling, the texture, the small shift in routine.

# IT IS OKAY TO ADMIT WHEN YOU ARE TIRED

conjure these mental images in the following order: one, a blue above-ground swimming pool filled with live anchovies in a midwestern backyard at dusk. two, a big boy restaurant from the perspective of a passenger in a car speeding down a highway illuminated by midday sun. three, a watercolor portrait of playboi carti. four, a key lime pie-flavored stick of lip balm. five, a red stepladder propped against an orange brick wall & a panting, slobbering st. bernard standing guard to the right of the stepladder. six, archival footage of the 1992 los angeles riots. seven, a gust of wind passing through a field of wheat after nightfall. eight, paste on paper. nine, a row of five slot machines, only the fourth of which being played by an elderly woman wearing a hawaiian shirt & cargo shorts, in an otherwise empty casino.

## "WE'RE A MIRACLE" BY CHRISTINA AGUILERA

i want to drive to a street i don't live on in a city i've never been to & sit on the sidewalk in front of a house that belongs to someone i don't know & use 25,000 sticks of chalk to draw a lifelike portrait of a caterpillar on the cement & when the stranger whose property i've chosen as my own personal art studio approaches me to ask who i am or what i think i'm doing i will simply point to the multicolored caterpillar portrait & say "that's you. that's what you look like."

# "MUST BE DREAMING" BY FROU FROU

at a wildlife sanctuary somewhere in kenya, there lives a young orphan elephant named maktao. maktao enjoys suckling from a rubber baby bottle filled with a special formula that is nutritionally similar to mother's milk. every day when it is feeding time, maktao gallops to the barn where he knows that a human caretaker will provide him with a bottle of formula. he takes the bottle from the caretaker in the barn & tilts the bottle upside down, his trunk wrapped around the mouth of the bottle while formula drips down the corners of his own mouth. the caretaker laughs at how happy & excited maktao is to feed. i laugh too, watching maktao on a computer screen somewhere else in the world. i feel connected to maktao & wish him well as he continues to grow & mature. maktao & i both know what it is to lose & to live with loss & to learn to find simple daily pleasures that help us grow & mature in spite of the absence of that which we have lost.

# "SELF V. FORMER SELF" BY KITTYHAWK

one sundrenched afternoon i open my bedroom door to step out into the hallway & in the hallway i find a dusty toy piano. i remember that i agreed to buy this toy piano from my roommate for twenty dollars. i bring the toy piano into my bedroom & use a swiffer cloth to dust it off. i play the opening notes of john cage's suite for toy piano. i place the toy piano in a corner of my bedroom beside my moroccan sintir, my stick bass, my yamaha keyboard, my circuit-bent casio. i make a lot of music that nobody listens to, but that's okay because i don't make it for anybody in particular. i step out of my bedroom & into the hallway & forget the reason why i wanted to leave my bedroom in the first place.

# WITH GNATS YOUR ARMS HAVE SAID SMOOTH LINES

with gnats // next journey

your arms // the stones

have said // stomach bile

smooth lines // like a

sad pity // peanut butter

bad behavior // aquarian burst

moon shades // how moist

blue suit // nearly dry

a landscape // under sea

of the // civilization has

hand my // lips pink

good reasons // chlorophyll hangs

or incantations // begins to

your heart // difficult time

talking about // every day

someone with // even light

they say // black waves

an eye // curious readers

for holding // dirty spit

like hands // what words

silence of // slit arms

cold air // half-moons joined

i'm trying // in blue

weeping & // neon shocks

being fustigated // always soft

spilled so // as fur

my mother // any subject

she sings // hours spent

so wildly // blowing on

the fable // its dismantling

# OXTAIL STEW & OCEAN BEHIND ME

oxtail stew & // & small catastrophes

ocean behind me // the corner house

the perfect word // through the windows

quick to melt // bushes & asphalt

mound of dirt // in the rain

the black steps // hot ochered light

in troubled times // her moon-cold shoulder

# AUTUMN BLUE SMOKE

autumn // plastic

blue // football

smoke // halted

turning // frozen

mist // longing

# BRITNEY'S BLACKOUT: A CENTO IN FIFTEEN PARTS

i.

gimme, gimme (more)

gimme, gimme (more)

gimme (more)

even when we're up against the wall

(give me more!)

ii.

i'm mrs. 'oh my god, that britney's shameless'

i'm mrs. 'oh my god, that britney's shameless'

i'm mrs. 'oh my god, that britney's shameless'

piece of me

(you want a piece of me?)

iii.

confidence is a must

animal in the sack

when you walk (when you walk)

and when you talk (when you talk)

got you on my radar


iv.

baby, i can make you feel

turn the lights down low if ya wanna

allow me to get you right

baby, i can make you feel

that's what i'm saying


v.

your lips, you're fine, you're heaven on earth

tell me that i'll always be the one that you want

take me back to that place in time

images of you occupy my mind

your perfect skin, your perfect smile

vi.

quarter past three, i'm ready to leave the party

get naked, get naked, get naked, get naked

i just want to take it off, i just want to take it off

i get the feeling that i just wanna be with ya

as long as you want it, come with me


vii.

it's a crazy night, let's make a, make a freakshow

it's all about me & you, doing how we do

said me & my girls 'bout to get it on

grab us a couple boys to go

we can give 'em a peepshow, peepshow


viii.

oh, toy soldier

i'm out the door, it's automatic, simple, babe

won't be just coming over

yeah, smash on the radio, bet i penned it!

oh, toy soldiers

ix.

yeah, yeah, yeah, yeah, yeah

i'm just too cool

if you've ever been to heaven, this is twice as nice

i'll take you higher

break it down, break it down, break it down


x.

yeah, yeah

i can feel you on my lips

you're filling me up

i can feel you on my lips

baby (baby), baby (baby), baby


xi.

i can't get enough of you

you make me feel so hot

uh-huh...

better hurry up, 'cause time is ticking, yeah

pull up to my bumper

xii.

my friends said you would play me, but i just said
they're crazy

just take it all as a sign that we're through
(goodbye)

it's time for me to get it on (okay)

it's time for me to move along (goodbye)

i'm tired of singing sad songs (alright)


xiii.

i love how you put me first

baby, feel my every word

there'll always be a song about you

how i'm your girl & you're my man

please turn up your radio

xiv.

body shaking, aching, i can't take it

everybody, come on, get to jumping

everybody

everybody, come on, let's keep grinding

everybody, feel the temperature rising


xv.

boy, don't play it safe

you might think i'm crazy

what you come here for?

danja, bring it back

oh, no (here we go)

## CAMPFIRE SONG

(again & again [tipsy lamps

glimmering sound  within your eyes

pushes through you)  burn there

(gay prelude  in the grass]

to a touch) [a light

(your lips  between two winds]

waxing & waning  [dove-soft night]

wadeable moons)  [hands of water

(little pink embers  open up

drift down)  & grasp mine]

# CANOPY COVER

*& i have been a tree's wide branches*

*as you look up along the way*

*& it seems to me believing*

*as i am see-through & sinking*

*& even more it seems a reason*

*by the doorways & the stairs*

*& the vases in the breezes*

*to let the fire grow out like hair*

        — thanksgiving, "responsibility"


tongue-out-of-cheek // test-your-might

the mountaintop conforms // contorts

like a rubber nipple // under baby's gums

baby yoda eyes // kit fisto smile

tentacool hair flowing // a tornado warning

the verbs in an example // of zeugma

these are the // features i picture

when i hear // the notes in your name

like hearing // al pacino yelling "great ass!"

or a tiny tune // ribcage-as-xylophone gag

I;m thinking about thos Bones // the bark

above // the root system

over another empty bowl // i'm listening

to your song // but the walkman skips

socking me // as would a hitmonchan

# MOVIES THAT I CAN REMEMBER WATCHING IN MY HIGH SCHOOL FILM STUDIES CLASS, 2009-2010

*(mostly in no particular order)*

the godfather (1972)

the godfather part ii (1974)

indiana jones & the temple of doom (1984)

indiana jones & the kingdom of the crystal skull (2008)

transformers (2007)

transformers: revenge of the fallen (2009)

who framed roger rabbit (1988)

e.t. the extra-terrestrial (1982)

the shining (1980)

cujo (1983)

juno (2007)

stagecoach (1939)

chinatown (1974)

breaking away (1979)

the hurt locker (2009)

# MOVIES THAT I CAN REMEMBER HATING WHILE WATCHING

*(in no particular order)*

the big bounce (2004)

transformers (2007)

transformers: revenge of the fallen (2009)

cats (2019)

the lion king (2019)

bewitched (2005)

joker (2019)

the santa clause 3: the escape clause (2006)

silver linings playbook (2012)

charlie and the chocolate factory (2005)

remember the titans (2000)

boat trip (2002)

grown ups (2010)

grown ups 2 (2013)

ghosts of mars (2001)

pirate radio (2009)

the heartbreak kid (2007)

the longest yard (2005)

the dukes of hazzard (2005)

across the universe (2007)

a christmas carol (2009)

the interview (2014)

some like it hot (1959)

## ALL MY FRIENDS ARE DEAD // EVERYONE IS MY FRIEND

some friends left because of geography

some friends left because of ideology

some friends left because their favorite tv show was about to start

some friends left because the dogs of my music howled too loud

some friends left because i asked them to leave

some friends left because

some friends left because i started being me

& they hated the color painted all over my fresh & happy self

some friends left because they found an easier type of love

some friends left because they wanted more of a challenge

some friends left because they wanted to kiss me & i never noticed

some friends left because we kissed

some friends left because i was so desperately afraid of them leaving

some friends left because their bodies stopped breathing


some of those friends made their bodies stop breathing via acupuncture

some of those friends left on accident & some left on purpose


some friends left & then came back

some friends left & can never return


troubled hearts truly do map deserts

may we all make it home safely

# FUCKING A STRANGER TWICE MY AGE IN THE BACK OF A GREYHOUND BUS EN ROUTE TO CLEVELAND

> *fucking strangers feels better,*
>
> *feels better fucking strangers*
>
> — joan of arc, "ne mosquitoes pass."

there are plenty of lonesome faggot hearts

beneath the surface of the sea


like cops' corpses in the dirt

making themselves useful as compost


after another night

of swiping right to silence


i think of him showing me

pictures of his younger self in drag


i touch myself to my memory

warm phantom feelings

dual-type fairy & ghost

hitting me hard & critical


a mental slideshow of hazy gazes

seeming more & more like memes


like me to my dad when he came out as a trump
supporter:

"why would you say something so controversial
yet so brave?"


or me when the man old enough to be my dad

asked if he could suck my cock & spit my cum into


my mouth:

"ok, boomer"

# "GAS STATION" BY YOUNG NUDY

why can't the lyrics be about a trans woman? ~ a
trans woman who has a thing for diamonds &
men who wear them? ~ a trans woman who might
tweet a selfie with the caption "#hotgirlsummer"?
~ who sticks herself with a two-inch needle once
a week? ~ who isn't interested in bottom surgery?
~ who has been a sex worker or a bartender? ~
who has been unemployed & homeless? ~ who
has slept in a parked car with no heat in the dead
of december? ~ who once worked in retail but was
fired because of baseless customer complaints? ~
who used to have a sugar daddy almost three
times her age? ~ who grew up yearning for the
touch of a man & feeling terrified by that want? ~
who loves smoking weed but also depends on it?
~ who worries about dying before the age of 30?
~ why can't the lyrics be about a woman rejected
by most? ~ why can't the lyrics be about a woman
rising like a glowing phoenix from the flames that
try to engulf her?

# THE BROKEN TOWER, REBUILT

*(after hart crane)*

the bell-rope that gathers god at dawn
dispatches me as though i were an
animal crossing a darkened marsh
towards shelter, heat, refuge.

sissy hypno is the opiate of the masses.
after work, i stand entranced by the void
of my broken bathroom sink, which
the landlord has promised to fix but has not.

the landlord promises simple maintenance
just as the boss promises a raised wage—
promises like seeds of everything i could be
without my labor exploited,

my heart halo'd by unearthed unrest,
my fatuous maw clawed open with
the force of a carillon's chime
while the bell-rope sways in finite jest

and i choke on the challenges of every day,

my tongue a cute, pink, dumbass worm.

what i mean to say is i know i deserve better

than the whims of this current cosmic timeline.


i deserve real sleep, real health, real salvation,

a functional sink, & a new set of colored pencils.

# RAINBOW ROAD

on my way to a friend's house, i drive past a
rainbow flag

then another, & another

& then three more rainbow flags


some of the rainbow flags are displayed outside of
people's houses

& some of them are displayed outside of
bars/restaurants


& i still feel like i wouldn't feel welcome in any of
those buildings


not because the people in those buildings would
harass or attack me for wearing makeup

a blouse

a skirt


but because they would probably just view me as
cis

as male


they would look at me & smile & say "#FKH8"

& i would look back at them & say

"your rainbow flags are empty corporate vessels

blank, blank signs"


i would say

"trans revolution over cis assimilation"


& then they would all call me a faggot

# A POEM ABOUT SPENDING A DAY WITH PAIN

*may 2019*

i wake up. i read about
the murder of muhlaysia
booker while sitting in
my bed. i get ready for
work. i shave. i shower.
i decide to wear lipstick
but not concealer. i show
up to work. i work. i read
a text from my friend alex,
who wants to start a local
trans militia. i tell them
about the new knife that
i recently bought. i buy
a bottle of cherry pop for
89 cents. i leave work. i
cook dinner. i read a book
of poems by morgan parker
while listening to drone music.

i watch the press conference

that chelsea manning gave

before returning to jail.

i brush blue dye into my hair

and tie a plastic grocery

bag around my scalp.

i read about the murder of

catalina casquete holguín

while sitting in my bed.

i fall asleep & dream of

people walking down streets

without being looked at

or followed or touched.

i dream of there being

no need for knives.

i dream of my cold hand

gripping my new knife

and running it through

my dyed-blue hair.

# MY MAIN NEW YEAR'S RESOLUTION IS TO POLICE MY OWN THOUGHT-CRIMES

i try not to think too much because thinking always leads to depression

thinking about my life for too long feels like a form of self-injury


i think i like the idea of children more than i like children themselves

children tend to say whatever they think


i like when a child says something quirky & unexpected

like a kid in a miranda july story


*me & you & everyone we know*

is a pretty good movie but the trailer is ten times better than the actual movie me & you & everyone we know

are all hurting but that's okay because we're here
to help each other heal


or at least that's what we try to do

i think

# VISIBILITY

they (pl.) see me (sing.)

dripping in velvet pencil skirt

blood the color of skylie jenner

concealer-smeared mouth-corners

toothy rose-thorn smile to match the crown

a musty mist of anti-androgen in the atmosphere

chipped paint/polish surrounded by wolfbitten skin

tight-knotted wigglytuff-pink hair-tie makes ponytail

demin flower blouse buttoned up to semi-shaven chest

lavender hammer next to aquatic palette in black tote bag

clutched while walking with shadowed eyes straight ahead

# MIRRORS ARE MEANT TO BE ONLY GLANCED AT, NEVER STARED INTO

in bed i turn to face my phone like a lover

i open facebook & think about tinder dates at age 27


i look at a meme about waluigi running for president

i watch a video of staten island cops planting drugs in a black man's car


i close my eyes for a moment & feel wildfire behind them

the space heater behind my head kicks on & off


in the bathroom mirror my beard begins to grow back

mere seconds after shaving


the sensation of razor burn lets me know i've tried my best

to avoid being called "sir" at work all day

but the five o'clock shadow is indeed a shadow

a ghost that is always somewhere in the haunted
house


i take a deep breath & plug my ears

*i'm on deebo lit // i'm on migo lit // i'm on kilo lit*

# MY FAVORITE POEM IS "MAD SCIENCE" BY PIGLET; MY SECOND-FAVORITE IS THE POEM THAT YOU DEDICATED TO ME BEFORE YOU DIED

i can read it in every jpeg of smiling you

eyeing with my little i

milk-breath in the morning

the ontology of sleeping in

a mewtwo-shaped cloud of ghost

flixster subscription renewed but unused


now i sit in my bed & on buses & next to tree stumps alone & i feel it


i don't care if a chest belongs to a man or a woman or a person who is neither

i just want to press my ear against it & listen to another life

while fingers toy with my hair simply because that's the thing to do

a car drove directly into me while i was driving a
different car one night

and i'm still not 100% sure that i didn't die
immediately


if i didn't, then why can i only see shades of
purple?


ooouuu!

# EACH DAY IS DIFFERENT & THE SAME AS COCKS

figure of fall-colored fatedness pitying broken
miracle's scattered gargoyles crumbling carefully
in heavy collapse & powdery oblivion trickling
whole flower-bright mountains bright lamp asses
inside boombox benevolence buried beside body
of flamingo shit kicked into one frank fantasy a
tomb unharassed swells slippery like something
under full-drawn fire viral metaphor for peeling
foothills suddenly small & weeping thrust thus
brushed along that thrift of heart that begins to
bear branches bending towards craggy zigzag
rockslides sixfold underthings opening spring
lashings above summered twilight sunlight now
alien like a white rainwind kitchening oak faces
no skin cellophane hybrid but gelatin snowfall all
drizzle & deathless clinging confetti this
strawberry flexi-script screendoor shrieking into
silence within shaded seconds body-boats wet
with out-fished morphine beauty parallel to
capital the sky classified as quixotic window
waiting for nothing & chains cut cloth with king-
size knife lollipop glow-worm candlelight
outspread like godfire against violets imitating
drenched bread the moon stained with skeleton
dust july gem flowerings withholding cellophane
beauty mysterious & familiar green apple glories
slapping rhinestone waters old molten eyes arise
from clay figure gray leafmold an easily aghast
pendulum shining glistening so slick & tireless no
frozen kindnesses no emeralds screaming in
shame melodrama alive against destiny sky-silent
salmon flicking lickety-split skitter thicker
thumbnail greasy with ocean's great shadowed
filth weather provokes weathervane blue-green &
boggy the absence of intended pattern wolfing

folds of light over orange canyons slender &
melancholy earth alone upturned frost-spackled
dramatically itself like papaya or oreo dark with
white disney stories lifted from whispery lips
something smudged fuck language sucked
swampcunt up buckle of monkeys their ancestors
tacked to clouds lifetimes of sleep suddenly
undone deleted dead blue-edged bloom noodles
nocturnal dooms carved from trees tall as
tattooed doodle dresses tight taste of missionary
breath breadth of heaven dog-toothed scarecrows
sleep silent dream things which j;u;n;g;l;e beyond
night into miracles tender & immortal steadily
shuffling from storm to casket sealed shut &
numbered with amber a nickelodeon's stylized
babyskin scrambles raven-winged upward
towards utmost drift tactful like the winter-maker
seeking spring flowerlike particles littering the
land mid-poem refusing to let up lawlessness
unlike anything else a cre-ma-tor-eum lullaby
memorized by heart hatless sea shadows hidden
deep enough in pulp of snail such speed flashing
flesh fatly slapped sleepy legs loosen inward
sunken sudden burn of sweat along limb-
twitched scrambles tantalizing wonderment
tornados rising a rumble returns nectar to grass
cloud cover showering scraps of rubble rubble
dazzle tranquil vintners citronella faggots
awaiting golden garden goodness a sapling of
hope hooking orphaned angels perfumed with
words of painted fields sheltering scavengers
resembling ballyhooed basket-work sirens
alarmed by sky slime hillside outcry outrang
against sacred fossils finally peppered across
queer coolness & into ancient body wrinkling yet
uninflected counting hands ears eyes wide tongue
pulled lips ever-so-slightly bloody sallowed
residue left behind & beautiful x a & x as a piston-
powered windowledge wind-wrought under
timbers softly swaying limber aflame upfloating

merely sowing stung defunct lavender loathing everybody's roots singing ghostthings conceive secret vacation finger with november sky welcoming greener sleep as puddle-wonderful flower-soft flopslump sonofabitch slim smell of moonly merciful swingthings neither too blossoming nor too moon gay-be-gay angels find crumbs of humble mysteries glimpsed by rugged faces tenderly eagerly wreathed with rind immemorial murmurs bright & numerable knowledgeable morning mountains oceaning imagination as something completely absolute a wholeness wildness just surface blooms craving nineteenth-century foliage formed from disembodied disassembled clouds finely-nerved mechanoreceptors alphabetti experiments in syllables flibberti pink plonk sliver-thin heads pullulating against gravity the open plywood heart of loneliness candles akin to bonfires warm as a sunburst crossing territories burning red & clean an obelisk reaped from shatter like sunstruck weeds or sun-bleached books left out in the common room full of furious stupor superstitions potent with heartbreak blood & dark a kiss pressed against demon earth bewitchingly thick against dirt flavored with egg flesh a root-ball thot alternating between addict-like obstructions & acute metacarpals masculine tongue outsources knot huhuhu fume & fulcrum stone-flagged blues sing a little louder

# WINE POEM

i'm shaking the virtually empty bottle of rosé so
that every last drop fills the floral coffee cup as i
switch from neil young's "philadelphia" to playboi
carti's "magnolia" because it's a friday night & for
once i don't have to spend it working my soulless,
thankless minimum-wage job so instead i've been
spending it on drinking this cheap wine from
walgreens & talking to my friends about the
systemic similarities between covid & aids, how
the people in power care so little & how their
apathy is by design, but now my friends have gone
to bed & it's just me again & thus i'm changing
lanes from depression-drinking to party-
drinking, piano ballads to soundcloud cyphers,
banging my head in time with the beat as best as
i can, & once the bottle is finally truly empty & the
mug is finally truly full i must resist the urge to
throw the bottle of barefoot against my bedroom
wall just because i want to shatter glass because i
feel like shattered glass might change something
& maybe it would in some other context but in the
context of me being alone in my apartment &
forgetting what it feels like to give my best friend
a hug, the more practical praxis is to sit here &
turn up the volume & count myself lucky to be
able to breathe at all.

# UNDERSTANDING IN A CAR CRASH

i'm sitting in the front lobby of the library where i work, an open book in my lap, my legs crossed under a long pink skirt, when i suddenly hear the long drone of a car horn followed by a simultaneous crunch & thud. i look up from one of ross gay's essays on delight & see through one of the ceiling-to-floor windows a classic fender-bender. a little silver & red coke-can mini-cooper has rear-ended a sleek gray jeep. from yards away i watch a silent dialogue between the two drivers, who are assessing the damage to both vehicles, which looks thankfully minimal to me, & gesturing back & forth in ways that indicate "are you okay?" & "yeah, i'm good" before the jeep owner points to a nearby marathon station for them to pull into. i watch both people step back into their cars & flow with the river of traffic towards the gas stop, where a similar chaplinesque dialogue starts up again, probably about insurance. i'm reminded of the last time i was rear-ended in traffic, which was not that long ago. it happened at a red light on my way to work, the split second after the light had turned green. the driver who bumped me showed me a stack of papa john's pizzas in his passenger seat while explaining how one had slid off the top of the tower & directly onto his lap, thus leading to the love-tap. we were both fine & so were our cars, & instead of swapping insurance info, the deliveryman offered me all the cash tips he'd made that night & his phone number along with the promise to smoke me out sometime. about a month later, i still haven't hit him up, but i don't think i need to, because calm post-accident exchanges full of apologies & concerns &

handshakes (safely metaphorical or dangerously real) are a delight that can provide its own sort of high.

# A MOMENT SUSPENDED IN TIME

i'm sitting in a blacklit corner of the local rollerena, watching the passing sk8r bois who look like girls, wanting to kiss their studded lips, hook a finger around their neon checkered belts, run a hand through their carefully tussled manic-panic'd hair, meet their guylined eyes with my own. i'm probably 14 or 15 years old & the year is probably 2005 or 2006 & i've come to this place to show support for my friend's band that covers songs by bands that all the boys who look like girls like. i'm looking at all the girl-boys & thinking about how i wish i could be a boy-girl. i've never worn even the mildest makeup despite my desire to do so so desperately. i hardly make eye contact with mirrors & try not to think about my body because not paying attention to it feels so much easier. i like some of the music made by the girlish boys on mtv2 because it includes screaming. i'm a pretty quiet kid & i don't know what would come out of me if i tried to scream. i don't know if i would like whatever i heard. another muffled song ends & a friend waves me over to the air hockey table behind the stage. the boys & girls on their skates keep circling around & around & around.

## YES, TRANSNESS IS A PATHOLOGY

b/c why else would anyone ever be trans in this world?

b/c i as a trans person always feel sick with hope

b/c my gender festers like a wound


one time i dedicated a whole book of poems to someone

& then that someone evaporated into a fogbow

so i crossed out their name in every author copy i sold


one time i drove behind a car with a vanity plate reading

"U2LATE"

which really resonated with me on an existential level


i spent my childhood playing nintendo 64 &

trying to settle into this unruly

body labelled "boy"

now i spend my adulthood playing nintendo 64

& trying to identify this still-ill body

whose label i have scraped away

## POEM TO BE READ AT ANY PACE OVER SILVER MT. ZION'S "BROKEN CHORDS CAN SING A LITTLE"

blood. i said :: blood! i cried

my body :: my blood

became :: an unruly roar

the radio beside :: my blood

was :: weeping

my brain waved :: goodbye

kissed a kiss :: colored dots

on a face :: marooned blue

against beige :: light

bat boy dyke :: snorlax fag

crossed out the eyes :: nbd

up up on :: the cold red roof

of your :: car parked car

happy birthday blunts :: peach pit

suite for toy piano :: blood music

the music of my blood :: pink

noise & carpeting :: wildfires

windblown :: over our windows

chili beans on :: the stove

in the kitchen :: air of coffee

gnats :: circling a drain

beans boiled :: my blood simmered

most at home :: with the tv on

my blood :: my blouse

prettied with marooning :: stains

# SIMILE

love is a faith a farm

love is a face a farm


love is a face a fish

love is a face a fence


love is a fear a fence

love is a love a fence


love is a love a swing

love is a love a song


love is a scream a song

love is a dream a song


love is a dream a tree

love is a dream a train


love is a pain a train

love is a hate a train

love is a hate a hit

love is a hate a wind


love is a need a wind

love is a weed a wind


love is a weed a needle

love is a weed a candle


love is a frown a candle

love is a friend a candle


love is a friend a canyon

love a friend a surgeon


love is a sense a surgeon

love is a self a surgeon


love is a self a sadness

love is a self a sonnet

# BEAUTIFUL PEOPLE'S SELFIES DON'T FLOP ON SOCIAL MEDIA

i wear my trans ugliness like a badge of honor.

sure, all trans people are ugly in the eyes of cis people,

but i am too ugly even for my siblings in transness

to like my selfies on twitter.

i don some freshly gay apparel ~

a blouse from ebay, shorts from goodwill

~ & strike a playful pose, painted

fingers flashing peace.

what was once ~ fleetingly ~

affirming of my femininity & fashion sense

now sits digitally dormant,

pixels for the pretty people to scoff at & scroll past.

i thank all of these people for reminding me

that i weigh 240 lbs,

that no amount of foundation can conceal all of
my facial hair,

that my palsied legs are unsexy in their
asymmetry,

etc, etc ~ all the ways one's body fails to belong...


thank you & fuck you

& the thousands of erect statues who follow you.


i drape myself in my trans ugliness

like valentino haute couture or

a velvet wedding veil,

as i marry the ever-spiteful spotlight

familiar to certain faggots like me ~

those of us who don't even fit the bill of faggotry.

# BREAKFAST

*& i believe*

*that when we die, we die*

*so let me love you tonight*

*let me love you tonight*

— the drums, "book of revelation"


my sister once told me, "it's a beautiful feeling
to wake up next to someone you love every m
orning. i know that you don't know that feelin
g, but…" she didn't know that i do know that
feeling ~ i wake up beside myself all the time,
all the pieces of me that are oh messy & oh lov
able, the cake of last night's makeup, the gelatin
of a gender wobbling towards womanhood. . . .
alone & in-love, i stumble then rise on each aw
kward morning, 13 mirrors standing guard roun
d the side of my bed ~ model #gbnnx0600022.
i have coffee with my transfemininity, make sm
all talk about the wrongs & rights of my body,
the weather as unpredictable as anything else. i
know what it is to sit with love, let it bubble up

& blow around. some mornings i wake up & t

here's a bird in the tree outside my window ~

that is love as well.

# MY FIVE FAVORITE STORIES BY ANNIE PROULX IN DESCENDING ORDER

tits-up in a ditch

the bunchgrass edge of the world

brokeback mountain

the mud below

people in hell just want a drink of water

# OF GRAMMAR OTHERWIS'E

*in memory of peter*

g[r]a[v]    x[c]a[v]a[t]n[g]    f[t]p[a]t[h]
s[m]c[r]c[l]    g[r]m[p]y    [s]t[r]a[t]c[a]s[t]r
[l]n[c]h[t]m    [s]l[m]n    [h]s[p]t[a]l    [n]s[l]a[t]n
[c]f[f]    a[b]s[t]r[a]c[t]n[s]    a[s]s[m]p[t]n[s]
t[r]t[p]s    [a]t[s]m    [r]s[s]t    [g]m[t]r[c]    m[a]n[l]a
[a]n[a]t[m]c[a]l[l]y    [n]c[r]s[s]s    [t]t[l]
a[l]a[r]m    [g]a[r]a[g]    m[a]g[c]a[l]    s[m]w[h]r
[s]f[f]c    [m]c[r]w[a]v    [y]l[l]w    [n]w[l]y[w]d
[b]a[c]k[s]a[t]    f[a]b[r]c    [c]p[b]r[d]    s[l]n[c]
r[a]r[v]w    [b]a[s]b[a]l[l]    a[t]l[a]s
[n]f[l]a[t]a[b]l    [m]a[l]b[x]    v[a]r[n]s[h]
g[a]l[a]x[y]   r[a]d[b]l[c]k   [c]a[f]t[r]a   [d]r[z]z[l]
y[a]r[b]k    [m]a[p]q[s]t    [c]a[r]c[a]t[r]
h[a]r[d]c[v]r    [f]n[g]r[n]a[l]    l[k]w[a]r[m]
b[l]a[c]k    [m]v[s]    p[l]a[s]t[c]    b[a]n[a]n[a]
b[r]r[t]    l[p]s[t]c[k]    c[a]m[r]a[m]a[n]
n[g]h[t]t[m]    x[t]r[n]a[l]    t[r]a[s]h[c]a[n]
s[w]a[t]s[h]r[t]    a[s]h[s]    g[m]m[y]
c[a]s[a]b[l]a[n]c[a]  m[a]c[r]b[t]c  [d]a[r]r[h]a
[d]v[d]    p[r]a[n]h[a]s    [s]w[t]z[r]l[a]n[d]
d[d]b[a]l[l]    p[a]r[a]g[r]a[p]h[s]    b[r]n[z]
m[r]t[g]a[g]    s[t]a[n]l[s]s    [m]x[r]    b[a]b[y]
s[l]a[n]d    [c]r[s]s[w]r[d]    c[m]p[t]r
[a]n[y]t[h]n[g]    m[r]n[n]g    [b]a[n]d[a]d
[c]l[c]k[w]r[k]   h[a]l[l]w[n]   n[j]r[y]   s[v]n[t]s
[n]d[r]g[r]n[d]    b[x]n[g]    a[l]l[g]a[t]r
[f]l[l]a[x]t[n]    [r]s[t]r[s]    m[t]h[r]
m[a]s[s]a[c]h[s]t[t]s  [c]a[r]t[r]d[g]  d[a]m[m]t
[s]t[r]a[w]b[r]r[y]    m[a]k[s]h[f]t    [b]a[r]f[t]
s[h]t[h]a[d]s    [s]a[r]c[a]s[m]    f[r]a[r]m    [t]t[l]
l[a]n[d]d    [b]t[t]r    [v]n[d]n[g]    l[b]w    [b]k[n]s

[n]c[n]t[r]l[l]a[b]l[y] w[h]l[c]h[a]r [m]n[p]l[y]
d[r]v[w]a[y]        c[c]p[d]        c[l]a[r]s[s]a
[s]p[r]a[d]s[h]t[s] h[a]n[d]l[b]a[r]s [b]c[y]c[l]
v[t]n[a]m[s]    m[z]a[k]    h[a]w[a]a[n]    t[w]x
[s]t[n]w[a]l[l] c[m]m[n] n[w]s[p]a[p]r [f]r[t]h
[v]a[c]a[n]t            [p]s[y]c[h]a[n]a[l]y[s]s
[a]s[s]h[l]s        [b]a[r]t[n]        s[h]p[s]h[l]y
[x]a[n]d[r]    a[f]t[r]n[n]    c[n]v[r]s[a]t[n]s
[j]w[l]r[y]    b[r]t[h]d[a]y    [c]a[r]d[b]a[r]d
[m]m[m]y    [t]g[h]t[n]s[s]        p[d]a[t]d
[d]s[c]n[n]c[t]n    [d]a[m]n[d]    h[l]l[y]w[d]
p[r]g[r]s[s]    c[l]w[n]f[s]h    [n]b[c]k[l]d
[c]l[d]l[s]s    [v]h[m]n[t]l[y]        j[g]g[n]g
[p]n[d]l[m]    t[n]s[t]    s[a]a[c]    a[n]t[h]l[l]
w[a]t[r]s[s]    v[r]c[r]w[d]d    [b]z    [f]r[n]a[c]
p[a]n[h]a[n]d[l]n[g]        c[h]r[s]        h[n]y
[g]r[a]d[a]t[d] b[t]t[n]s [b]a[c]k[b]n [m]t[n]g
[s]t[a]g[n]a[n]t        [c]b[c]l        [n]r[v]a[n]a
[b]a[r]s[t]a [r]b[t] m[s]s[n]g[r] c[r]n[k]l[d]
f[x]a[t]n    [s]p[r]s[s]    n[g]h[t]    n[c]k[l]a[c]
s[p]a[r]k[l]    s[x]    a[d]v[n]t[r]s    [p]c[n]c
[c]h[r]s[t]m[a]s[s]        p[h]a[r]m[a]c[y]
k[n]d[r]g[a]r[t]n            [a]n[n]v[r]s[a]r[y]
f[l]r[s]c[n]t    [a]s[s]s[t]a[n]t    [h]a[d]p[h]n[s]
c[n]v[y]r    [t]a[d]p[l]s    [c]l[a]s[s]r[m]
n[a]m[p]l[a]t    [p]a[q]    s[g]t[t]    c[l]p[b]a[r]d
[c]c[p]d    [p]h[n]x    [p]r[j]d[c]    h[a]t[w]a[v]
d[y]s[f]n[c]t[n]a[l]            s[p]r[a]d[s]h[t]s
[w]a[d]l[w]    w[r]s[t]w[a]t[c]h    [r]r[p]r[s]s[b]l
[m]n[s]y[l]l[a]b[c]    r[s]l[t]s    [d]a[r]k[n]s[s]
g[r]a[d]a[t]n        [n]t[r]n[t]        a[s]y[l]m
[w]a[s]h[n]g[t]n    [a]t[p]l[t]        n[a]p[k]n
[f]l[a]s[h]b[a]c[k]    m[a]h[g]a[n]y    [n]
m[c]r[w]a[v]d [n]s[l]y [x]c[t]m[n]t [a]t[m]a[l]
p[l]a[y]g[r]n[d]    a[t]t[a]    a[n]y[t]h[n]g
[s]n[l]g[h]t [t]a[n]g[l]d [n]s [s]a[t]r[d]a[y]s
[l]g[c]a[l]l[y]  a[s]s[h]l  [n]a[s]s  [s]k[l]t[n]
p[a]s[s]a[g]w[a]y[s]        s[y]m[t]r[c]a[l]l[y]

h[a]l[l]w[a]y [h]r[r]d[l]y [s]p[a]c [s]n[a]p[p]d
[n]a[v]y [m]a[r]b[l] t[x]t[b]k [h]a[n]d[s]m
[r]h[y]t[h]m[c] g[m]n [a]t[t]n[d]a[n]t
[p]a[r]a[c]h[t]s [h]m [n]d[r]s[d] f[n]g[r]t[p]s
[a]r[p]l[a]n [g]r[l]f[r]n[d] f[l]m[m]a[k]r[s]
n[w]s[l]t[t]r[s] f[r]k [a]s[p]h[a]l[t] y[s]c[k]t[s]
p[c]t[r] t[v] p[a]j[a]m[a]s [s]c[l]p[t]r
[t]p[p]r[w]a[r] s[w]m[s]t[s] p[r]c[l]a[n]
d[s]r[d]r [t]m[m]y [f]r[p]l[a]c [l]v
[c]n[g]r[a]t[l]a[t]n[s] h[m]m[a]d
[s]h[a]l[y]n[n] c[s]t[a]l[a] l[a]n[g]a[g] p[l]l[w]
g[d]d[a]m[n]d [g]r[a]n[d]s [a]b[n]r[m]a[l]t[y]
m[t]h[r] l[p]r[c]h[a]n [y]a[n]k[d] b[l]b[r]r[s]
m[a]g[c]a[l] f[l]t[t]r[d] p[a]s[s]n[g]r
[m]l[k]s[h]a[k]s [t]a[t]t[n]g [g]n[t]n [a]w[a]y
[g]r[a]n[d]c[h]l[d]r[n] m[n]k[y] c[g]a[r]t[t]s
[n]s [d]r[w]a[y] d[s]m[s]s[a]l [g]r[a]n[l]a
[p]r[g]n[a]n[t] s[w]a[l]l[w]d [x]a[m]p[l]
f[n]a[n]c[a]l [a]w[s]m [r]v[s]n[g]
n[a]t[r]a[l]n[s]s [s]t[a]t[m]n[t] v[l]n[t]l[y]
h[y]p[r]b[l] s[y]m[b]l[s]m [b]l[a]t[a]n[c]y

# TWO EXAMPLES OF WHEN THE POETRY JUST HAPPENS AROUND YOU IN REAL TIME

i.

an old man walked into the library

with an ancient portable computer ~

one of those desktops built into a briefcase

from before the rise of laptops ~

& booted it up & tried

to access the public wifi

through a dial-up connection,

& just as the screams & squelches of

the dial-up blared through the library,

a great storm charged into the city

with its own scream of thunder.


ii.

40 minutes later,

i was driving home through the same storm

while listening to

"pictures of success" by rilo kiley

& thinking about all my dead friends,

including but not limited to my dad.

# MY GENDER AUTOCOMPLETED

my gender is a little late today

my gender & i are still rookies in the near future

my gender understands the rug in your bathroom
on the back of the toilet

my gender asks for three references other than
previous employers or relatives who live in
trailers & it's not intentional or malicious

my gender can figure something out at some
point

my gender has been pretty busy for me

my gender likes to be a good roommate

my gender says "where do you live now?"

my gender wants to date me & i don't know what
you did

my gender knows what kind of goofballs will be out & about with you


my gender goes to sleep & has a dream & the language is meant to mimic the language of dreams but there's not really any hidden meaning or secret code


my gender may be a few minutes late today

# CYCLICAL (1)

it feels so special to me,

sleepaddled at the plot

or the tooloud sound

of the themself then there—


the attic, where carmen is

so very excited to be

a particular somethingness:


nirvana, however it be known...


'action' appears innately

for the other.


i walk back to remind myself why

and i return to it,

a total of disquiet.


nothing may dwell within me.

# CYCLICAL (2)

nothingness leads to

what is incomplete.


a splintered pine, yellowing—


now it's none?


perversity in the ocean of human life,

close to the fire

of a computer screen, and


what language becomes

is perhaps

a bookbag full of rivals,

an axiom.


sometimes the night's

a merry one.


first time in years tonight.

## XERXES THE BLOWFISH

the blowfish:

it's less an ironic statement than a

battle between coyotes,

another trip on behalf of those

unhappiest moments never heard of...


this narrow thudding timeshaped face

has always been much more less prevalent,

more insecure and

curious, here

inside the sun's lifespan—


faintly falling,

filtered almost solely through the chest,

the same repeated experience of you

with no words of wanting me.

## ONE OF THE FEW BENEFITS OF BEING TRANSGENDER

i have become very, very good at hiding

# WHY I USED TO BITE MY FINGERNAILS

because i could not paint them

# SEVENTEEN ONE-WORD POEMS

1.

**why**

not

2.

**not**

okay

3.
**hoping**

still

4.
**happiness**

someday

5.
**bluish**

red

6.

**yellow**

screen


7.

**your**

smile


8.

**platonic**

love


9.

**memory**

petrichor


10.

**rarity**

quiet


11.

**bodies**

nuisances

12.
**image**

apparitional


13.
**never**

home


14.
**always**

elsewhere


15.
**hand**

gun


16.
**gun**

shot


17.

**title**

poem

# THE SKY IS ACTUALLY PURPLE

& every day is a poem worth publishing

# DAD

*how badly I want*

*my father to be resting,*

*and resting,*

*and smiling,*

*in the breathing,*

*and the breathing,*

*and surface with his nose*

*kissed with the gold*

*kissing lilies do...*

— Ross Gay, "Be Holding"

on the day of my dad's death, he could communicate to me only by squeezing my hand, our palms intertwined, mine a sauna, his a tundra. i wore a mask over my face and he wore a tube down his throat, his open mouth turned into a pool of red in which a single fly kept trying to swim. i swatted that fly away again and again and again while i talked to him, not about being trans but about being thankful for every time he lifted me up from the clutches of the dark or planted me firmly into the ground so as not to balloon away. he had done everything he could to protect himself and others from covid, but he had also been a smoker since the age of ten. his lungs were ready to be unrooted and balloon away. as he was too. time froze, thawed, bled out, and evaporated. then i let go of his hand and sat in another room until a doctor came and said, "he's ballooned away, in the sky now. we watched him until the sun stopped us from looking. he might be the sun now."

# BLUE ICE

ice-blue

blue ice

ice-blue

blue ice


ice-blue

blue ice


ice-blue

blue ice


ice-blue


blue ice


ice-blue


blue ice


ice-blue

blue ice

ice-blue

blue ice


ice-blue

blue ice

ice-blue

blue ice


ice-blue

blue ice


ice-blue

blue ice


ice-blue


blue ice


ice-blue


blue ice

# ACKNOWLEDGEMENTS

"mobile television (a)," "mobile television (b)," "solstice sonnet (summer)," and "solstice sonnet (winter)" originally appeared in *UndergroundBooks*.

"we are only as we are," "movies directed by amy heckerling," and "it is okay to admit when you are tired" originally appeared in *Gold Wake Live*.

"britney's blackout: a cento in fifteen parts" originally appeared in *Be About It Zine*.

"canopy cover" originally appeared in *Futures Trading*.

"all my friends are dead // everyone is my friend" and "my main new year's resolution is to police my own thought-crimes" originally appeared in *Philosophical Idiot*.

"fucking a stranger twice my age in the back of a greyhound bus en route to cleveland" and "'gas station' by young nudy" originally appeared in *Marlskarx*.

"visibility" and "a moment suspended in time" originally appeared in *Witch Craft Magazine*.

"poem to be read at any pace over silver mt. zion's 'broken chords can sing a little'" originally appeared in *goodbaad.*

"simile" and "of grammar otherwiS'e" originally appeared in *experiential-experimental-literature.*

"my gender autocompleted" and "beautiful people's selfies don't flop on social media" originally appeared in *Dream Pop.*

"breakfast" originally appeared in *Voicemail Poems.*

"cyclical (1)," "cyclical (2)," and "xerxes the blowfish" originally appeared in *what i would say* (Peanut Gallery Press).

"one of the few benefits of being transgender" and "why i used to bite my fingernails" originally appeared in *In Between Hangovers.*

The seventeen one-word poems originally appeared in *Brave New Word.*

# MORE TITLES FROM
# BE ABOUT IT PRESS

*I've Been On Tumblr* by Jesse Prado, 2014

*Bye, Product* by Catch Breath, 2015

*Paper Flowers, Invisible Birds* by Amy Saul-Zerby, 2017

*I Love You, It Looks Like Rain* by June Gehringer, 2018

*Disaster Horse: Smol Essays* by Nooks Krannie, 2019

*A Pretty Little Wilderness* by Cassandra Dallett, 2020

*Be A Bough Tit* by Richard Loranger, 2020

*Double Rainbow* by Lonely Christopher, 2021

*Blueberry Lemonade* by Marzi Margo, 2021

*Broken: A Life of Aileen Wuornos in 33 Poems* by Natasha Dennerstein, 2021


Find out more on our website!

beaboutitpress.com

Follow @baipress on twitter

Marzi Margo is a person who writes and resides in Cleveland, Ohio. Ver other books include pink maggit america (Ghost City Press, 2022) and Blueberry Lemonade (Be About It Press, 2021). Ve tweets about poetry, gender, video games, and being tired @wigglytuff_pink.

www.ingramcontent.com/pod-product-compliance
Lightning Source LLC
Chambersburg PA
CBHW031630040426
42452CB00007B/756